CW01081318

THE
POCKET

Love Poems

Published in 2025
by Gemini Books
Part of Gemini Books Group

Based in Woodbridge and London

Marine House, Tide Mill Way
Woodbridge, Suffolk IP12 1AP
United Kingdom
www.geminibooks.com

Text and Design © 2025 Gemini Adult Books Ltd
Part of the Gemini Pockets series

Cover image: Shutterstock/Oliko; The Graphics Fairy
Compiled by Becky Miles

ISBN 978-1-78675-182-9

All rights reserved. No part of this publication may be reproduced in
any form or by any means – electronic, mechanical, photocopying,
recording or otherwise – or stored in any retrieval system of any
nature without prior written permission from the copyright holders.

A CIP catalogue record for this book is available from the British Library.

Disclaimer: The book is a guidebook purely for information and
entertainment purposes only. All trademarks, individual and company
names, brand names, registered names, quotations, celebrity names,
logos, dialogues and catchphrases used or cited in this book are the
property of their respective owners. The publisher does not assume
and hereby disclaims any liability to any party for any loss, damage
or disruption caused by errors or omissions, whether such errors or
omissions result from negligence, accident or any other cause. This
book is an unofficial and unauthorized publication by Gemini Adult
Books Ltd and has not been licensed, approved, sponsored or endorsed
by any person or entity.

Printed in China

10 9 8 7 6 5 4 3 2 1

Images: Sabelskaya/Shutterstock.com 4; all others courtesy of Freepik.

THE
POCKET

Love Poems

G:

Contents

Introduction

As timeless as the stars, love has been a favourite subject of poets since humans first began to communicate their feelings in written form thousands of years ago. Whether that love be eternal, romantic, sensual or doomed in some way, poets have given voice to our deepest emotions in their love poems, expressing beautifully the sentiments we so often struggle to articulate.

In this collection, you'll find poems that explore all aspects of this most powerful 'affliction', including some of the most famous love poems of them all. Immerse yourself and enjoy.

Chapter One

Eternal Love

A Letter to Her Husband, absent upon Publick employment

My head, my heart, mine Eyes, my life, nay, more,
My joy, my Magazine of earthly store,
If two be one as surely thou and I,
How stayest thou there, whilst I at Ipswich lye?
So many steps, head from the heart to sever
If but a neck, soon would we be together;
I like the earth this season, mourn in black
My Sun is gone so far in's Zodiack,
Whom whilst I 'joyed, nor storms, nor frosts I felt,
His warmth such frigid colds did cause to melt.
My chilled limbs now nummed lye forlorn,
Return, return sweet Sol from Capricorn;

In this dead time, alas, what can I more
Than view those fruits which through thy heat I bore?
Which sweet contentment yield me for a space,
True, living Pictures of their Fathers face.
O strange effect! now thou art Southward gone,
I weary grow, the tedious day so long;
But when thou Northward to me shalt return,
I wish my Sun may never set but burn
Within the Cancer of my glowing breast,
The welcome house of him my dearest guest.
Where ever, ever stay, and go not thence,
Till nature's sad decree shall call thee hence;
Flesh of thy flesh, bone of thy bone,
I here, thou there, yet both but one.

Anne Bradstreet

Bright Star

Bright star, would I were stedfast as thou art—
    Not in lone splendour hung aloft the night
And watching, with eternal lids apart,
    Like nature's patient, sleepless Eremite,
The moving waters at their priestlike task
    Of pure ablution round earth's human shores,
Or gazing on the new soft-fallen mask
    Of snow upon the mountains and the moors—
No—yet still stedfast, still unchangeable,
    Pillow'd upon my fair love's ripening breast,
To feel for ever its soft fall and swell,
    Awake for ever in a sweet unrest,
Still, still to hear her tender-taken breath,
And so live ever—or else swoon to death.

John Keats

I Loved You First: But Afterwards Your Love

I loved you first: but afterwards your love
Outsoaring mine, sang such a loftier song
As drowned the friendly cooings of my dove.
Which owes the other most? my love was long,
And yours one moment seemed to wax more strong;
I loved and guessed at you, you construed me
And loved me for what might or might not be—
Nay, weights and measures do us both a wrong.
For verily love knows not 'mine' or 'thine;'
With separate 'I' and 'thou' free love has done,
For one is both and both are one in love:
Rich love knows nought of 'thine that is not mine;'
Both have the strength and both the length thereof,
Both of us, of the love which makes us one.

Christina Rossetti

Sudden Light

I have been here before,
But when or how I cannot tell:
I know the grass beyond the door,
The sweet keen smell,
The sighing sound, the lights around the shore.
You have been mine before,—
How long ago I may not know:
But just when at that swallow's soar
Your neck turn'd so,
Some veil did fall,—I knew it all of yore.
Has this been thus before?
And shall not thus time's eddying flight
Still with our lives our love restore
In death's despite,
And day and night yield one delight once more?

Dante Gabriel Rossetti

Sonnets from the Portuguese 14

If thou must love me, let it be for nought
Except for love's sake only. Do not say
I love her for her smile ... her look ... her way
Of speaking gently, ... for a trick of thought
That falls in well with mine, and certes brought
A sense of pleasant ease on such a day'—
For these things in themselves, Belovèd, may
Be changed, or change for thee,—and love, so wrought,
May be unwrought so. Neither love me for
Thine own dear pity's wiping my cheeks dry,—
A creature might forget to weep, who bore
Thy comfort long, and lose thy love thereby!
But love me for love's sake, that evermore
Thou may'st love on, through love's eternity.

Elizabeth Barrett Browning

Love and Friendship

Love is like the wild rose-briar,
Friendship like the holly-tree—
The holly is dark when the rose-briar blooms
But which will bloom most constantly?

The wild rose-briar is sweet in spring,
Its summer blossoms scent the air;
Yet wait till winter comes again
And who will call the wild-briar fair?

Then scorn the silly rose-wreath now
And deck thee with the holly's sheen,
That when December blights thy brow
He still may leave thy garland green.

Emily Brontë

It was a quiet way

It was a quiet way—
He asked if I was his—
I made no answer of the Tongue
But answer of the Eyes—
And then He bore me on
Before this mortal noise
With swiftness, as of Chariots
And distance, as of Wheels.
This World did drop away
As Acres from the feet
Of one that leaneth from Balloon
Upon an Ether street.
The Gulf behind was not,
The Continents were new—
Eternity it was before
Eternity was due.
No Seasons were to us—
It was not Night nor Morn—
But Sunrise stopped upon the place
And fastened it in Dawn.

Emily Dickinson

Friendship

I think awhile of Love, and while I think,
    Love is to me a world,
    Sole meat and sweetest drink,
    And close connecting link
        Tween heaven and earth.

I only know it is, not how or why,
    My greatest happiness;
    However hard I try,
    Not if I were to die,
        Can I explain.

I fain would ask my friend how it can be,
    But when the time arrives,
    Then Love is more lovely
    Than anything to me,
        And so I'm dumb.

For if the truth were known, Love cannot speak,
    But only thinks and does;
    Though surely out 'twill leak
    Without the help of Greek,
        Or any tongue.

A man may love the truth and practise it,
    Beauty he may admire,
    And goodness not omit,
    As much as may befit
        To reverence.

But only when these three together meet,
    As they always incline,
    And make one soul the seat,
    And favorite retreat,
        Of loveliness;

When under kindred shape, like loves and hates
    And a kindred nature,
    Proclaim us to be mates,
    Exposed to equal fates
        Eternally;

And each may other help, and service do,
    Drawing Love's bands more tight,
    Service he ne'er shall rue
    While one and one make two,
        And two are one;

In such case only doth man fully prove
    Fully as man can do,
    What power there is in Love
    His inmost soul to move
      Resistlessly.

—

Two sturdy oaks I mean, which side by side,
    Withstand the winter's storm,
    And spite of wind and tide,
    Grow up the meadow's pride,
      For both are strong

Above they barely touch, but undermined
    Down to their deepest source,
    Admiring you shall find
    Their roots are intertwined
      Insep'rably.

Henry David Thoreau

Love One Another

Love one another, but make not a bond of love:
Let it rather be a moving sea between the shores of
    your souls.
Fill each other's cup, but drink not from one cup.
Give one another of your bread, but eat not from the
    same loaf.
Sing and dance together and be joyous, but let each one
    of you be alone.
Even as the strings of a lute are alone though they
    quiver with the same music.
Give your hearts, but not into each other's keeping.
For only the hand of Life can contain your hearts.
And stand together yet not too near together:
For the pillars of the temple stand apart,
And the oak tree and the cypress grow not in each
    other's shadow.

Kahlil Gibran

The Sun Rising

Busy old fool, unruly sun,
     Why dost thou thus,
Through windows, and through curtains call on us?
Must to thy motions lovers' seasons run?
     Saucy pedantic wretch, go chide
     Late school boys and sour prentices,
  Go tell court huntsmen that the king will ride,
  Call country ants to harvest offices,
Love, all alike, no season knows nor clime,
Nor hours, days, months, which are the rags of time.

     Thy beams, so reverend and strong
     Why shouldst thou think?
I could eclipse and cloud them with a wink,
But that I would not lose her sight so long;
     If her eyes have not blinded thine,
     Look, and tomorrow late, tell me,
  Whether both th' Indias of spice and mine
  Be where thou leftst them, or lie here with me.
Ask for those kings whom thou saw'st yesterday,
And thou shalt hear, All here in one bed lay.

She's all states, and all princes, I,
Nothing else is.
Princes do but play us; compared to this,
All honour's mimic, all wealth alchemy.
Thou, sun, art half as happy as we,
In that the world's contracted thus.
Thine age asks ease, and since thy duties be
To warm the world, that's done in warming us.
Shine here to us, and thou art everywhere;
This bed thy centre is, these walls, thy sphere.

John Donne

Song of Love XXIV

I am the lover's eyes, and the spirit's
Wine, and the heart's nourishment.
I am a rose. My heart opens at dawn and
The virgin kisses me and places me
Upon her breast.

I am the house of true fortune, and the
Origin of pleasure, and the beginning
Of peace and tranquility. I am the gentle
Smile upon his lips of beauty. When youth
Overtakes me he forgets his toil, and his
Whole life becomes reality of sweet dreams.

I am the poet's elation,
And the artist's revelation,
And the musician's inspiration.

I am a sacred shrine in the heart of a
Child, adored by a merciful mother.

I appear to a heart's cry; I shun a demand;
My fullness pursues the heart's desire;
It shuns the empty claim of the voice.

I appeared to Adam through Eve
And exile was his lot;
Yet I revealed myself to Solomon, and
He drew wisdom from my presence.

I smiled at Helena and she destroyed Tarwada;
Yet I crowned Cleopatra and peace dominated
The Valley of the Nile.

I am like the ages—building today
And destroying tomorrow;
I am like a god, who creates and ruins;
I am sweeter than a violet's sigh;
I am more violent than a raging tempest.

Gifts alone do not entice me;
Parting does not discourage me;
Poverty does not chase me;
Jealousy does not prove my awareness;
Madness does not evidence my presence.

Oh seekers, I am Truth, beseeching Truth;
And your Truth in seeking and receiving
And protecting me shall determine my
Behaviour.

Kahlil Gibran

For Some We Loved

For some we loved, the loveliest and the best
That from His vintage rolling Time hath pressed,
Have drunk the Cup a round or two before,
And one by one crept silently to rest.

Omar Khayyam

Music, When Soft Voices Die

Music, when soft voices die,
Vibrates in the memory—
Odours, when sweet violets sicken,
Live within the sense they quicken.

Rose leaves, when the rose is dead,
Are heaped for the belovèd's bed;
And so thy thoughts, when thou art gone,
Love itself shall slumber on.

Percy Bysshe Shelley

Annabel Lee

It was many and many a year ago,
In a kingdom by the sea,
That a maiden there lived whom you may know
By the name of Annabel Lee;
And this maiden she lived with no other thought
Than to love and be loved by me.

I was a child and she was a child,
In this kingdom by the sea:
But we loved with a love that was more than love—
I and my Annabel Lee—
With a love that the wingèd seraphs of Heaven
Coveted her and me.

And this was the reason that, long ago,
In this kingdom by the sea,
A wind blew out of a cloud, chilling
My beautiful Annabel Lee;
So that her highborn kinsman came
And bore her away from me,
To shut her up in a sepulchre
In this kingdom by the sea.

The angels, not half so happy in Heaven,
Went laughing at her and me—
Yes!—that was the reason (as all men know,
In this kingdom by the sea)
That the wind came out of the cloud by night,
Chilling and killing my Annabel Lee.

But our love it was stronger by far than the love
Of those who were older than we—
Of many far wiser than we—
And neither the angels in Heaven above,
Nor the demons down under the sea,
Can ever dissever my soul from the soul
Of the beautiful Annabel Lee.

For the moon never beams, without bringing me dreams
Of the beautiful Annabel Lee;
And the stars never rise, but I feel the bright eyes
Of the beautiful Annabel Lee;
And so, all the night-tide, I lie down by the side
Of my darling—my darling—my life and my bride,
In her sepulchre there by the sea,
In her tomb by the sounding sea.

Edgar Allan Poe

Unending Love

I seem to have loved you in numberless forms,
     numberless times…
In life after life, in age after age, forever.
My spellbound heart has made and remade the
     necklace of songs,
That you take as a gift, wear round your neck in your
     many forms,
In life after life, in age after age, forever.

Whenever I hear old chronicles of love, it's age-old pain,
It's ancient tale of being apart or together.
As I stare on and on into the past, in the end you emerge,
Clad in the light of a pole-star, piercing the darkness
     of time.
You become an image of what is remembered forever.

You and I have floated here on the stream that brings
    from the fount.
At the heart of time, love of one for another.
We have played alongside millions of lovers,
Shared in the same shy sweetness of meeting,
the same distressful tears of farewell,
Old love but in shapes that renew and renew forever.

Today it is heaped at your feet, it has found its end
    in you
The love of all man's days both past and forever:
Universal joy, universal sorrow, universal life.
The memories of all loves merging with this one love
    of ours—
And the songs of every poet past and forever.

Rabindranath Tagore

Give All to Love

Give all to love;
Obey thy heart;
Friends, kindred, days,
Estate, good fame,
Plans, credit, and the Muse,—
Nothing refuse.

'Tis a brave master,
Let it have scope:
Follow it utterly,
Hope beyond hope:
High and more high
It dives into noon,
With wing unspent,
Untold intent:
But 'tis a god,
Knows its own path
And the outlets of the sky.

'Tis not for the mean,
It requireth courage stout,
Souls above doubt,
Valor unbending;
Such 'twill reward,
They shall return
More than they were,
And ever ascending.

Leave all for love;
Yet, hear me, yet,
One word more thy heart behoved,
One pulse more of firm endeavor,
Keep thee to-day,
To-morrow, for ever,
Free as an Arab
Of thy beloved.

Cling with life to the maid;
But when the surprise,
Vague shadow of surmise
Flits across her bosom young,
Of a joy apart from thee,
Free be she, fancy-free,
Do not thou detain her vesture's hem,
Nor the palest rose she flung
From her summer diadem.

Though thou loved her as thyself,
As a self of purer clay,
Tho' her parting dims the day,
Stealing grace from all alive;
Heartily know,
When half-gods go,
The gods arrive.

Ralph Waldo Emerson

A Moment of Happiness

A moment of happiness,
you and I sitting on the verandah,
apparently two, but one in soul, you and I.
We feel the flowing water of life here,
you and I, with the garden's beauty
and the birds singing.
The stars will be watching us,
and we will show them
what it is to be a thin crescent moon.
You and I unselfed, will be together,
indifferent to idle speculation, you and I.
The parrots of heaven will be cracking sugar
as we laugh together, you and I.
In one form upon this earth,
and in another form in a timeless sweet land.

Rumi

Love

We two that planets erst had been
Are now a double star,
And in the heavens may be seen,
Where that we fixed are.
Yet whirled with subtle power along,
Into new space we enter,
And evermore with spheral song
Revolve about one centre.

Henry David Thoreau

Sonnet 18

Shall I compare thee to a summer's day?
Thou art more lovely and more temperate:
Rough winds do shake the darling buds of May,
And summer's lease hath all too short a date:
Sometime too hot the eye of heaven shines,
And often is his gold complexion dimmed;
And every fair from fair sometime declines,
By chance, or nature's changing course, untrimmed:
But thy eternal summer shall not fade,
Nor lose possession of that fair thou ow'st;
Nor shall Death brag thou wander'st in his shade
When in eternal lines to time thou grow'st:
    So long as men can breathe or eyes can see,
    So long lives this, and this gives life to thee.

William Shakespeare

William Shakespeare
(1564–1616)

'Sonnet 18' is arguably the most famous of Shakespeare's sonnets, which were published together in a single volume in 1609. In this collection of 154 poems – a sonnet is a poem of 14 lines – the vast majority are addressed to an unnamed young man, or 'fair youth', by the admiring poet.

The sonnet cycle begins with the poet urging the fair youth to marry and start a family, before moving on to describe the deep affection held by the poet for his friend. There follows a series of romantic betrayals by the youth, including with a mysterious married woman known as the 'Dark Lady', with whom the poet himself also becomes involved.

The sonnet describes the great beauty of the fair youth by first comparing it to a perfect summer's day. It then immortalizes this beauty by stating that while a summer's day will fade and pass, the youth's perfection will live on in the lines of the sonnet, even as he, too, will age and die.

There has been much speculation over the years as to the identities of the figures in the sonnets but there is no real evidence to suggest they were real rather than fictional characters.

Passion

When I look back
On days already lived
I am content.
For I have laughed
With the dew of morn,
The calm of night;
With the dawn of youth
And spring's bright days.
Mid-summer's bloom
And autumn's ripening glory
My youth rejoiced.
And when winter bleak
Spread melancholy 'round
I still smiled on.
And I have loved
With quivering arms that

Clung, and throbbing breast —
With all the white-hot blood
Of mating's flaming urge.
My cool, white soul
Has oft fared forth
In Astral ways,
for none may lag
When star dust hides the earth.
The wing of dreams
Have swept me up
To touch my feed on cloud
And wander where none
But souls dare climb.

Zora Neale Hurston

Chapter Two

Romantic Love

When I Heard at the Close of the Day

When I heard at the close of the day how my name had
been receiv'd with plaudits in the capitol, still it was
not a happy night for me that follow'd,
And else when I carous'd, or when my plans were
accomplish'd, still I was not happy,
But the day when I rose at dawn from the bed of
perfect health, refresh'd, singing, inhaling the ripe
breath of autumn,
When I saw the full moon in the west grow pale and
disappear in the morning light,
When I wander'd alone over the beach, and undressing
bathed, laughing with the cool waters, and saw the
sun rise,
And when I thought how my dear friend my lover was
on his way coming, O then I was happy,

O then each breath tasted sweeter, and all that day
    my food nourish'd me more, and the beautiful day
    pass'd well,
And the next came with equal joy, and with the next at
    evening came my friend,
And that night while all was still I heard the waters roll
    slowly continually up the shores,
I heard the hissing rustle of the liquid and sands as
    directed to me whispering to congratulate me,
For the one I love most lay sleeping by me under the
    same cover in the cool night,
In the stillness in the autumn moonbeams his face was
    inclined toward me,
And his arm lay lightly around my breast—and that
    night I was happy.

Walt Whitman

She Walks in Beauty

She walks in beauty, like the night
Of cloudless climes and starry skies;
And all that's best of dark and bright
Meet in her aspect and her eyes;
Thus mellowed to that tender light
Which heaven to gaudy day denies.

One shade the more, one ray the less,
Had half impaired the nameless grace
Which waves in every raven tress,
Or softly lightens o'er her face;
Where thoughts serenely sweet express,
How pure, how dear their dwelling-place.

And on that cheek, and o'er that brow,
So soft, so calm, yet eloquent,
The smiles that win, the tints that glow,
But tell of days in goodness spent,
A mind at peace with all below,
A heart whose love is innocent!

George Gordon, Lord Byron

Lord Byron
(1788–1824)

The larger-than-life figure of George Gordon, Lord Byron, was a leading light of the Romantic artistic movement of the early nineteenth century, which emphasized subjectivity and the feelings of the individual. Famously remembered by one of his many lovers as being 'mad, bad and dangerous to know', he remains a beloved English poet as well as a folk hero in Greece, where he fought against the Ottomans in the Greek War of Independence.

'She Walks in Beauty' is one of Byron's most famous works and has been the inspiration for many artists and composers over the years. It is said to have been written the night after a party in the summer of 1814, where Byron had met one Anne Wilmot, who was wearing dark mourning clothes, and was struck by her uncommon beauty. Anne was the wife of Byron's cousin, Sir Robert Wilmot, and although there is nothing to suggest that she and Byron were lovers, this poem gives the reader a palpable sense of the power of instant attraction.

The Passionate Shepherd to His Love

Come live with me and be my love,
And we will all the pleasures prove,
That Valleys, groves, hills, and fields,
Woods, or steepy mountain yields.

And we will sit upon the Rocks,
Seeing the Shepherds feed their flocks,
By shallow Rivers to whose falls
Melodious birds sing Madrigals.

And I will make thee beds of Roses
And a thousand fragrant posies,
A cap of flowers, and a kirtle
Embroidered all with leaves of Myrtle;

A gown made of the finest wool
Which from our pretty Lambs we pull;
Fair lined slippers for the cold,
With buckles of the purest gold;

A belt of straw and Ivy buds,
With Coral clasps and Amber studs:
And if these pleasures may thee move,
Come live with me, and be my love.

The Shepherds' Swains shall dance and sing
For thy delight each May-morning:
If these delights thy mind may move,
Then live with me, and be my love.

Christopher Marlowe

Sonnets from the Portuguese 43

How do I love thee? Let me count the ways.
I love thee to the depth and breadth and height
My soul can reach, when feeling out of sight
For the ends of being and ideal grace.
I love thee to the level of every day's
Most quiet need, by sun and candle-light.
I love thee freely, as men strive for right;
I love thee purely, as they turn from praise.
I love thee with the passion put to use
In my old griefs, and with my childhood's faith.
I love thee with a love I seemed to lose
With my lost saints. I love thee with the breath,
Smiles, tears, of all my life; and, if God choose,
I shall but love thee better after death.

Elizabeth Barrett Browning

Elizabeth Barrett Browning
(1806–1861)

Influential Victorian poet, Elizabeth Barrett
Browning started writing poems at the age of eleven.
She published her first volume of poetry in 1838
and became hugely successful in her lifetime,
despite frequent and debilitating illness. Elizabeth's
work caught the attention of poet and playwright
Robert Browning and, despite her father's intense
disapproval, the two corresponded, courted,
fell in love and secretly married in 1846.

Elizabeth's father disinherited her and the couple
moved to Italy, where they had a son, and remained
there until Elizabeth died in Florence in 1861.

Sonnets from the Portuguese is a collection of love
poems that were written soon after Elizabeth met
Robert Browning and published to great acclaim in
1850. 'Sonnet 43' – the most famous – is one of many
that describe the poet's love for her new husband.
The title of the volume implies the sonnets may be
translations from Portuguese and this may have been
an attempt by the author to disguise their origin from
readers because of their deeply personal nature.

The Lovers

The rose did caper on her cheek,
Her bodice rose and fell,
Her pretty speech, like drunken men,
Did stagger pitiful.

Her fingers fumbled at her work,—
Her needle would not go;
What ailed so smart a little maid
It puzzled me to know,

Till opposite I spied a cheek
That bore another rose;
Just opposite, another speech
That like the drunkard goes;

A vest that, like the bodice, danced
To the immortal tune,—
Till those two troubled little clocks
Ticked softly into one.

Emily Dickinson

Marriage Bells

Music and silver chimes and sunlit air,
Freighted with the scent of honeyed orange-flower;
Glad, friendly festal faces everywhere.
She, rapt from all in this unearthly hour,
With cloudlike, cast-back veil and faint-flushed cheek,
In bridal beauty moves as in a trance
Alone with him, and fears to breathe, to speak,
Lest the rare, subtle spell dissolve perchance.
But he upon that floral head looks down,
Noting the misty eyes, the grave sweet brow—
Doubts if her bliss be perfect as his own,
And dedicates anew with inward vow
His soul unto her service, to repay
Richly the sacrifice she yields this day.

Emma Lazarus

21

I love my love with a v
Because it is like that
I love my love with a b
Because I am beside that
A king.
I love my love with an a
Because she is a queen
I love my love and a a is the best of them
Think well and be a king,
Think more and think again
I love my love with a dress and a hat
I love my love and not with this or with that
I love my love with a y because she is my bride
I love her with a d because she is my love beside
Thank you for being there
Nobody has to care
Thank you for being here
Because you are not there.

And with and without me which is and without she she
can be late and then and how and all around we think
and found that it is time to cry she and I.

Gertrude Stein

Camomile Tea

Outside the sky is light with stars;
There's a hollow roaring from the sea.
And, alas! for the little almond flowers,
The wind is shaking the almond tree.

How little I thought, a year ago,
In the horrible cottage upon the Lee
That he and I should be sitting so
And sipping a cup of camomile tea.

Light as feathers the witches fly,
The horn of the moon is plain to see;
By a firefly under a jonquil flower
A goblin toasts a bumble-bee.

We might be fifty, we might be five,
So snug, so compact, so wise are we!
Under the kitchen-table leg
My knee is pressing against his knee.

Our shutters are shut, the fire is low,
The tap is dripping peacefully;
The saucepan shadows on the wall
Are black and round and plain to see.

Katherine Mansfield

Harlem Night Song

Come,
Let us roam the night together
Singing.
I love you.
Across
The Harlem roof-tops
Moon is shining
Night sky is blue.
Stars are great drops
Of golden dew.
In the cabaret
The jazz-band's playing.
I love you.
Come,
Let us roam the night together
Singing.

Langston Hughes

Juke Box Love Song

I could take the Harlem night
and wrap around you,
Take the neon lights and make a crown,
Take the Lenox Avenue buses,
Taxis, subways,
And for your love song tone their rumble down.
Take Harlem's heartbeat,
Make a drumbeat,
Put it on a record, let it whirl,
And while we listen to it play,
Dance with you till day—
Dance with you, my sweet brown Harlem girl.

Langston Hughes

For Myself Alone, I Would Not Be

For myself alone, I would not be
    Ambitious in my wish; but, for you,
    I would be trebled twenty times myself;
    A thousand times more fair,
    Ten thousand times more rich.

Louisa May Alcott

A Kiss on the Forehead

A kiss on the forehead—erases misery.
I kiss your forehead.

A kiss on the eyes—lifts sleeplessness.
I kiss your eyes.

A kiss on the lips—is a drink of water.
I kiss your lips.

A kiss on the forehead—erases memory.

Marina Tsvetaeva
(translated from the Russian by Ilya Kaminsky)

Recuerdo

We were very tired, we were very merry—
We had gone back and forth all night on the ferry.
It was bare and bright, and smelled like a stable—
But we looked into a fire, we leaned across a table,
We lay on a hill-top underneath the moon;
And the whistles kept blowing, and the dawn
    came soon.

We were very tired, we were very merry—
We had gone back and forth all night on the ferry;
And you ate an apple, and I ate a pear,
From a dozen of each we had bought somewhere;
And the sky went wan, and the wind came cold,
And the sun rose dripping, a bucketful of gold.

We were very tired, we were very merry,
We had gone back and forth all night on the ferry.
We hailed, 'Good morrow, mother!' to a shawl-covered
    head,
And bought a morning paper, which neither of us read;
And she wept, 'God bless you!' for the apples and pears,
And we gave her all our money but our subway fares.

Edna St. Vincent Millay

When I Too Long Have Looked Upon Your Face

When I too long have looked upon your face,
Wherein for me a brightness unobscured
Save by the mists of brightness has its place,
And terrible beauty not to be endured,
I turn away reluctant from your light,
And stand irresolute, a mind undone,
A silly, dazzled thing deprived of sight
From having looked too long upon the sun.
Then is my daily life a narrow room
In which a little while, uncertainly,
Surrounded by impenetrable gloom,
Among familiar things grown strange to me
Making my way, I pause, and feel, and hark,
Till I become accustomed to the dark.

Edna St. Vincent Millay

Love's Philosophy

The fountains mingle with the river
And the rivers with the ocean,
The winds of heaven mix for ever
With a sweet emotion;
Nothing in the world is single;
All things by a law divine
In one spirit meet and mingle.
Why not I with thine?—
See the mountains kiss high heaven
And the waves clasp one another;
No sister-flower would be forgiven
If it disdained its brother;
And the sunlight clasps the earth
And the moonbeams kiss the sea:
What is all this sweet work worth
If thou kiss not me?

Percy Bysshe Shelley

Romance

I will make you brooches and toys for your delight
Of bird-song at morning and star-shine at night.
I will make a palace fit for you and me
Of green days in forests and blue days at sea.

I will make my kitchen, and you shall keep your room,
Where white flows the river and bright blows the broom,
And you shall wash your linen and keep your body white
In rainfall at morning and dewfall at night.

And this shall be for music when no one else is near,
The fine song for singing, the rare song to hear!
That only I remember, that only you admire,
Of the broad road that stretches and the roadside fire.

Robert Louis Stevenson

Again and Again

Again and again, however we know the landscape
   of love
and the little churchyard there, with its sorrowing names,
and the frighteningly silent abyss into which the others
fall: again and again the two of us walk out together
under the ancient trees, lie down again and again
among the flowers, face to face with the sky.

Rainer Maria Rilke

A Red, Red Rose

O my Luve is like a red, red rose
That's newly sprung in June;
O my Luve is like the melody
That's sweetly played in tune.

So fair art thou, my bonnie lass,
So deep in luve am I;
And I will luve thee still, my dear,
Till a' the seas gang dry.

Till a' the seas gang dry, my dear,
And the rocks melt wi' the sun;
I will love thee still, my dear,
While the sands o' life shall run.

And fare thee weel, my only luve!
And fare thee weel awhile!
And I will come again, my luve,
Though it were ten thousand mile.

Robert Burns

Without Warning

Without warning
as a whirlwind
swoops on an oak
Love shakes my heart.

Sappho

Because

Oh, because you never tried
To bow my will or break my pride,
And nothing of the cave-man made
You want to keep me half afraid,
Nor ever with a conquering air
You thought to draw me unaware—
Take me, for I love you more
Than I ever loved before.
And since the body's maidenhood
Alone were neither rare nor good
Unless with it I gave to you
A spirit still untrammeled, too,
Take my dreams and take my mind
That were masterless as wind;
And 'Master!' I shall say to you
Since you never asked me to.

Sara Teasdale

Other Men

When I talk with other men
    I always think of you—
Your words are keener than their words,
    And they are gentler, too.
When I look at other men,
    I wish your face were there,
With its gray eyes and dark skin
    And tossed black hair.
When I think of other men,
    Dreaming alone by day,
The thought of you like a strong wind
    Blows the dreams away.

Sara Teasdale

The Wanderer

I saw the sunset-colored sands,
    The Nile like flowing fire between,
    Where Rameses stares forth serene,
And Ammon's heavy temple stands.
I saw the rocks where long ago,
    Above the sea that cries and breaks,
    Swift Perseus with Medusa's snakes
Set free the maiden white like snow.
And many skies have covered me,
    And many winds have blown me forth,
    And I have loved the green, bright north,
And I have loved the cold, sweet sea.
But what to me are north and south,
    And what the lure of many lands,
    Since you have leaned to catch my hands
And lay a kiss upon my mouth.

Sara Teasdale

The Letter

Little cramped words scrawling all over the paper
Like draggled fly's legs,
What can you tell of the flaring moon
Through the oak leaves?
Or of my uncertain window and the bare floor
Spattered with moonlight?
Your silly quirks and twists have nothing in them
Of blossoming hawthorns,
And this paper is dull, crisp, smooth, virgin
    of loveliness
Beneath my hand.

I am tired, Beloved, of chafing my heart against
The want of you;
Of squeezing it into little inkdrops,
And posting it.
And I scald alone, here, under the fire
Of the great moon.

Amy Lowell

He Wishes for the Cloths of Heaven

Had I the heavens' embroidered cloths,
Enwrought with golden and silver light,
The blue and the dim and the dark cloths
Of night and light and the half-light,
I would spread the cloths under your feet:
But I, being poor, have only my dreams;
I have spread my dreams under your feet;
Tread softly because you tread on my dreams.

W. B. Yeats

Chapter Three

Doomed Love

He would not stay for me, and who can wonder

He would not stay for me, and who can wonder?
   He would not stay for me to stand and gaze.
I shook his hand, and tore my heart in sunder,
   And went with half my life about my ways.

A. E. Housman
(From A Shropshire Lad*)*

XVIII: Oh, when I was in love with you

Oh, when I was in love with you,
Then I was clean and brave,
And miles around the wonder grew
How well did I behave.

And now the fancy passes by,
And nothing will remain,
And miles around they'll say that I
Am quite myself again.

A. E. Housman

Remember

Remember me when I am gone away,
    Gone far away into the silent land;
    When you can no more hold me by the hand,
Nor I half turn to go yet turning stay.
Remember me when no more day by day
    You tell me of our future that you plann'd:
    Only remember me; you understand
It will be late to counsel then or pray.
Yet if you should forget me for a while
    And afterwards remember, do not grieve:
    For if the darkness and corruption leave
    A vestige of the thoughts that once I had,
Better by far you should forget and smile
    Than that you should remember and be sad.

Christina Rossetti

Love Again Blues

My life ain't nothin'
But a lot o' Gawd-knows-what.
I say my life ain't nothin'
But a lot o' Gawd-knows-what.
Just one thing after 'nother
Added to de trouble that I got.

When I got you I
Thought I had an angel-chile.
When I got you
Thought I had an angel-chile.
You turned out to be a devil
That mighty nigh drove me wild!

Tell me, tell me,
What makes love such an ache and pain?
Tell me what makes
Love such an ache and pain?
It takes you and it breaks you—
But you got to love again.

Langston Hughes

Re-Voyage

What of the days when we two dreamed together?
    Days marvellously fair,
As lightsome as a skyward floating feather
    Sailing on summer air—
Summer, summer, that came drifting through
Fate's hand to me, to you.

What of the days, my dear? I sometimes wonder
    If you too wish this sky
Could be the blue we sailed so softly under,
    In that sun-kissed July;
Sailed in the warm and yellow afternoon,
With hearts in touch and tune.

Have you no longing to re-live the dreaming,
    Adrift in my canoe?
To watch my paddle blade all wet and gleaming
    Cleaving the waters through?
To lie wind-blown and wave-caressed, until
Your restless pulse grows still?

Do you not long to listen to the purling
    Of foam athwart the keel?
To hear the nearing rapids softly swirling
    Among their stones, to feel
The boat's unsteady tremor as it braves
The wild and snarling waves?

What need of question, what of your replying?
    Oh! well I know that you
Would toss the world away to be but lying
    Again in my canoe,
In listless indolence entranced and lost,
Wave-rocked, and passion tossed.

Ah me! my paddle failed me in the steering
    Across love's shoreless seas;
All reckless, I had ne'er a thought of fearing
    Such dreary days as these.
When through the self-same rapids we dash by,
My lone canoe and I.

Emily Pauline Johnson

La Belle Dame Sans Merci

Ah, what can ail thee, knight-at-arms,
Alone and palely loitering?
The sedge is wither'd from the lake,
And no birds sing.

Ah, what can ail thee, knight-at-arms,
So haggard and so woe-begone?
The squirrel's granary is full,
And the harvest's done.

I see a lily on thy brow,
With anguish moist and fever-dew,
And on thy cheek a fading rose
Fast withereth too.

I met a lady in the meads,
Full beautiful—a faery's child;
Her hair was long, her foot was light,
And her eyes were wild.

I made a garland for her head,
And bracelets too, and fragrant zone;
She look'd at me as she did love,
And made sweet moan.

I set her on my pacing steed,
And nothing else saw all day long,
For sidelong would she lean, and sing
A faery's song.

She found me roots of relish sweet,
And honey wild, and manna-dew,
And sure in language strange she said—
'I love thee true'.

She took me to her Elfin grot,
And there she wept and sighed full sore,
And there I shut her wild wild eyes
With kisses four.

And there whe lullèd me asleep,
And there I dreamed—Ah! woe betide!—
The latest dream I ever dreamt
On the cold hill side.

I saw pale kings, and princes too,
Pale warriors, death-pale were they all;
Who cried—'La Belle Dame sans Merci
Hath thee in thrall!'

I saw their starved lips in the gloam,
With horrid warning gapèd wide,
And I awoke, and found me here,
On the cold hill's side.

And this is why I sojourn here,
Alone and palely loitering,
Though the sedge is withered from the lake,
And no birds sing.

John Keats

John Keats
(1795–1821)

The powerfully evocative 'La Belle Dame sans Merci' ('The Beautiful Lady without Mercy') tells the story of wandering knight left wretched and bereft after an encounter with a mysterious elfin beauty. The knight recounts being entranced by the woman and taken to her grotto before falling asleep only to be troubled by nightmares warning him about her. He wakes alone and cuts a tragic, ailing figure when found looking for his love.

John Keats wrote this poem in 1819, just two years before his death from tuberculosis at the age of 25. He had been a published poet for less than four years but is now revered as one of the most significant of the Romantic movement. Keats had recently met and fallen deeply in love with 18-year-old Fanny Brawne, writing her hundreds of letters describing his ardent feelings. They became secretly engaged, but his status as a struggling poet and the onset of his illness meant they were unable to marry before his untimely death.

Keats' passion for Fanny, his desperate feelings of despondency about their situation and a preoccupation with death are reflected in 'La Belle Dame', which became widely known after his death. Often cited in art and literature, it is perhaps best known through several famous Pre-Raphaelite paintings of the same name.

Mary's Dream

The moon had climbed the eastern hill
Which rises o'er the sands of Dee,
And from its highest summit shed
A silver light on tower and tree,
When Mary laid her down to sleep
(Her thoughts on Sandy far at sea);
When soft and low a voice was heard,
Saying, 'Mary, weep no more for me.'

She from her pillow gently raised
Her head, to see who there might be,
And saw young Sandy, shivering stand
With visage pale and hollow e'e.
'Oh Mary dear, cold is my clay;
It lies beneath the stormy sea;
Far, far from thee, I sleep in death.
Dear Mary, weep no more for me.

'Three stormy nights and stormy days
We tossed upon the raging main.
And long we strove our bark to save;
But all our striving was in vain.
E'en then, when terror chilled my blood,
My heart was filled with love of thee.
The storm is past, and I'm at rest;
So, Mary, weep no more for me.

'Oh maiden dear, yourself prepare;
We soon shall meet upon that shore
Where love is free from doubt and care,
And you and I shall part no more.'
Loud crew the cock, the shadow fled;
No more her Sandy did she see;
But soft the passing spirit said,
'Sweet Mary, weep no more for me.'

Louisa May Alcott

Isolation: To Marguerite

We were apart; yet, day by day,
I bade my heart more constant be.
I bade it keep the world away,
And grow a home for only thee;
Nor fear'd but thy love likewise grew,
Like mine, each day, more tried, more true.

The fault was grave! I might have known,
What far too soon, alas! I learn'd—
The heart can bind itself alone,
And faith may oft be unreturn'd.
Self-sway'd our feelings ebb and swell—
Thou lov'st no more;—Farewell! Farewell!

Farewell!—and thou, thou lonely heart,
Which never yet without remorse
Even for a moment didst depart
From thy remote and spherèd course
To haunt the place where passions reign—
Back to thy solitude again!

Back! with the conscious thrill of shame
Which Luna felt, that summer-night,
Flash through her pure immortal frame,
When she forsook the starry height

To hang over Endymion's sleep
Upon the pine-grown Latmian steep.

Yet she, chaste queen, had never proved
How vain a thing is mortal love,
Wandering in Heaven, far removed.
But thou hast long had place to prove
This truth—to prove, and make thine own:
'Thou hast been, shalt be, art, alone.'

Or, if not quite alone, yet they
Which touch thee are unmating things—
Ocean and clouds and night and day;
Lorn autumns and triumphant springs;
And life, and others' joy and pain,
And love, if love, of happier men.

Of happier men—for they, at least,
Have dream'd two human hearts might blend
In one, and were through faith released
From isolation without end
Prolong'd; nor knew, although not less
Alone than thou, their loneliness.

Matthew Arnold

Longing

Come to me in my dreams, and then
By day I shall be well again!
For so the night will more than pay
The hopeless longing of the day.

Come, as thou cam'st a thousand times,
A messenger from radiant climes,
And smile on thy new world, and be
As kind to others as to me!

Or, as thou never cam'st in sooth,
Come now, and let me dream it truth,
And part my hair, and kiss my brow,
And say, My love why sufferest thou?

Come to me in my dreams, and then
By day I shall be well again!
For so the night will more than pay
The hopeless longing of the day.

Matthew Arnold

Ashes of Life

Love has gone and left me and the days are all alike;
Eat I must, and sleep I will,—and would that night
    were here!
But ah!—to lie awake and hear the slow hours strike!
Would that it were day again!—with twilight near!

Love has gone and left me and I don't know what to do;
This or that or what you will is all the same to me;
But all the things that I begin I leave before
    I'm through,—
There's little use in anything as far as I can see.

Love has gone and left me,—and the neighbors knock
    and borrow,
And life goes on forever like the gnawing of a mouse,—
And to-morrow and to-morrow and to-morrow
    and to-morrow
There's this little street and this little house.

Edna St. Vincent Millay

What Lips My Lips Have Kissed

What lips my lips have kissed, and where, and why,
I have forgotten, and what arms have lain
Under my head till morning; but the rain
Is full of ghosts to-night, that tap and sigh
Upon the glass and listen for reply,
And in my heart there stirs a quiet pain
For unremembered lads that not again
Will turn to me at midnight with a cry.
Thus in the winter stands the lonely tree,
Nor knows what birds have vanished one by one,
Yet knows its boughs more silent than before:
I cannot say what loves have come and gone,
I only know that summer sang in me
A little while, that in me sings no more.

Edna St. Vincent Millay

A Fragment

Beautiful star with the crimson lips
And flagrant daffodil hair,
Come back, come back, in the shaking ships
O'er the much-overrated sea,
To the hearts that are sick for thee
With a woe worse than mal de mer—
O beautiful stars with the crimson lips
And the flagrant daffodil hair.—
O ship that shakes on the desolate sea,
Neath the flag of the wan White Star,
Thou bringest a brighter star with thee
From the land of the Philistine,
Where Niagara's reckoned fine
And Tupper is popular—
O ship that shakes on the desolate sea,
Neath the flag of the wan White Star.

Oscar Wilde

Her Voice

The wild bee reels from bough to bough
    With his furry coat and his gauzy wing.
        Now in a lily-cup, and now
    Setting a jacinth bell a-swing,
        In his wandering;
Sit closer love: it was here I trow
    I made that vow,

Swore that two lives should be like one
As long as the sea-gull loved the sea,
As long as the sunflower sought the sun,—
It shall be, I said, for eternity
    'Twixt you and me!
Dear friend, those times are over and done,
    Love's web is spun.

Look upward where the poplar trees
Sway and sway in the summer air,
Here in the valley never a breeze
Scatters the thistledown, but there
    Great winds blow fair
From the mighty murmuring mystical seas,
    And the wave-lashed leas.

Look upward where the white gull screams,
    What does it see that we do not see?
Is that a star? or the lamp that gleams
    On some outward voyaging argosy,—
        Ah! can it be
We have lived our lives in a land of dreams!
        How sad it seems.

Sweet, there is nothing left to say
    But this, that love is never lost,
Keen winter stabs the breasts of May
    Whose crimson roses burst his frost,
        Ships tempest-tossed
Will find a harbour in some bay,
        And so we may.

And there is nothing left to do
    But to kiss once again, and part,
Nay, there is nothing we should rue,
    I have my beauty,—you your Art,
        Nay, do not start,
One world was not enough for two
        Like me and you.

Oscar Wilde

The Moment You Left Me

The moment you left me,
sweetness was stolen from my tongue.
I turned to wax, burned like a candle
all night, scorched by fire,
no honey.
No way to reach you,
no way to touch your beauty.
My body lies here in ruins.
My soul, a night owl.

Rumi
(translated by Haleh Liza Gafori)s

The Kiss

I hoped that he would love me,
    And he has kissed my mouth,
But I am like a stricken bird
    That cannot reach the south.
For though I know he loves me,
    To-night my heart is sad;
His kiss was not so wonderful
    As all the dreams I had.

Sara Teasdale

Ode to Aphrodite

Deathless Aphrodite, throned in flowers,
Daughter of Zeus, O terrible enchantress,
With this sorrow, with this anguish, break my spirit
Lady, not longer!

Hear anew the voice! O hear and listen!
Come, as in that island dawn thou camest,
Billowing in thy yoked car to Sappho
Forth from thy father's

Golden house in pity! … I remember:
Fleet and fair thy sparrows drew thee, beating
Fast their wings above the dusky harvests,
Down the pale heavens,

Lightning anon! And thou, O blest and brightest,
Smiling with immortal eyelids, asked me:
'Maiden, what betideth thee? Or wherefore
Callest upon me?

'What is here the longing more than other,
Here in this mad heart? And who the lovely
One beloved that wouldst lure to loving?
Sappho, who wrongs thee?

'See, if now she flies, she soon must follow;
Yes, if spurning gifts, she soon must offer;
Yes, if loving not, she soon must love thee,
Howso unwilling ...'

Come again to me! O now! Release me!
End the great pang! And all my heart desireth
Now of fulfillment, fulfill! O Aphrodite,
Fight by my shoulder!

Sappho

After Love

There is no magic any more,
    We meet as other people do,
You work no miracle for me
    Nor I for you.

You were the wind and I the sea—
    There is no splendor any more,
I have grown listless as the pool
    Beside the shore.

But though the pool is safe from storm
    And from the tide has found surcease,
It grows more bitter than the sea,
    For all its peace.

Sara Teasdale

I Love You

When April bends above me
And finds me fast asleep,
Dust need not keep the secret
A live heart died to keep.

When April tells the thrushes,
The meadow-larks will know,
And pipe the three words lightly
To all the winds that blow.

Above his roof the swallows,
In notes like far-blown rain,
Will tell the little sparrow
Beside his window-pane.

O sparrow, little sparrow,
When I am fast asleep,
Then tell my love the secret
That I have died to keep.

Sara Teasdale

I Approach,
and I Withdraw

I approach, and I withdraw:
who but I could find
absence in the eyes,
presence in what's far?

From the scorn of Phyllis,
now, alas, I must depart.
One is indeed unhappy
who misses even scorn!

So caring is my love
that my present distress
minds hard-heartedness less
than the thought of its loss.

Leaving, I lose more
than what is merely mine:
in Phyllis, never mine,
I lose what can't be lost.

Oh, pity the poor person
who aroused such kind disdain
that to avoid giving pain,
it would grant no favour!

For, seeing in my future
obligatory exile,
she disdained me the more,
that the loss might be less.

Oh, where did you discover
so neat a tactic, Phyllis:
denying to disdain
the garb of affection?

To live unobserved
by your eyes, I now go
where never pain of mine
need flatter your disdain.

Sor Juana Inés de la Cruz

Extract from
My Lady

My lady, I must implore
forgiveness for keeping still,
if what I meant as tribute
ran contrary to your will.

Please do not reproach me
if the course I have maintained
in the eagerness of my love
left my silence unexplained.

I love you with so much passion,
neither rudeness nor neglect
can explain why I tied my tongue,
yet left my heart unchecked.

The matter to me was simple:
love for you was so strong,
I could see you in my soul
and talk to you all day long.

With this idea in mind,
I lived in utter delight,
pretending my subterfuge
found favour in your sight.

In this strange, ingenious fashion,
I allowed the hope to be mine
that I still might see as human
what I really conceived as divine.

Oh, how mad I became
in my blissful love of you,
for even though feigned, your favour
made all my madness seem true!

Sor Juana Inés de la Cruz

A Thunderstorm in Town

She wore a 'terra-cotta' dress,
And we stayed, because of the pelting storm,
Within the hansom's dry recess,
Though the horse had stopped; yea, motionless
We sat on, snug and warm.

Then the downpour ceased, to my sharp sad pain,
And the glass that had screened our forms before
Flew up, and out she sprang to her door:
I should have kissed her if the rain
Had lasted a minute more.

Thomas Hardy

Love's Secret

Never seek to tell thy love,
Love that never told can be;
For the gentle wind does move
Silently, invisibly.

I told my love, I told my love,
I told her all my heart;
Trembling, cold, in ghastly fears,
Ah! she did depart!

Soon as she was gone from me,
A traveller came by,
Silently, invisibly
He took her with a sigh.

William Blake

Chapter Four

Sensual Love

In a Garden

Gushing from the mouths of stone men
To spread at ease under the sky
In granite-lipped basins,
Where iris dabble their feet
And rustle to a passing wind,
The water fills the garden with its rushing,
In the midst of the quiet of close-clipped lawns.

Damp smell the ferns in tunnels of stone,
Where trickle and plash the fountains,
Marble fountains, yellowed with much water.
Splashing down moss-tarnished steps
It falls, the water;
And the air is throbbing with it.
With its gurgling and running.
With its leaping, and deep, cool murmur.
And I wished for night and you.
I wanted to see you in the swimming-pool,
White and shining in the silver-flecked water.
While the moon rode over the garden,
High in the arch of night,
And the scent of the lilacs was heavy with stillness.

Night, and the water, and you in your whiteness, bathing!

Amy Lowell

To Celia

Drink to me only with thine eyes,
    And I will pledge with mine;
Or leave a kiss but in the cup,
    And I'll not look for wine.
The thirst that from the soul doth rise
    Doth ask a drink divine;
But might I of Jove's nectar sup,
    I would not change for thine.

I sent thee late a rosy wreath,
    Not so much honouring thee
As giving it a hope, that there
    It could not withered be.
But thou thereon didst only breathe,
    And sent'st it back to me;
Since when it grows, and smells, I swear,
    Not of itself, but thee.

Ben Jonson

Song

O Love! that stronger art than wine,
Pleasing delusion, witchery divine,
Wont to be prized above all wealth,
Disease that has more joys than health;
Though we blaspheme thee in our pain,
And of thy tyranny complain,
We are all bettered by thy reign.

What reason never can bestow
We to this useful passion owe;
Love wakes the dull from sluggish ease,
And learns a clown the art to please,
Humbles the vain, kindles the cold,
Makes misers free, and cowards bold;
'Tis he reforms the sot from drink,
And teaches airy fops to think.

When full brute appetite is fed,
And choked the glutton lies and dead,
Thou new spirits dost dispense
And 'finest the gross delights of sense:
Virtue's unconquerable aid
That against Nature can persuade,
And makes a roving mind retire
Within the bounds of just desire;
Cheerer of age, youth's kind unrest,
And half the heaven of the blest!

Aphra Behn

Valentine

Too high, too high to pluck
My heart shall swing.
A fruit no bee shall suck,
No wasp shall sting.

If on some night of cold
It falls to ground
In apple-leaves of gold
I'll wrap it round.

And I shall seal it up
With spice and salt,
In a carven silver cup,
In a deep vault.

Before my eyes are blind
And my lips mute,
I must eat core and rind
Of that same fruit.

Before my heart is dust
By the end of all,
Eat it I must, I must
Were it bitter gall.

But I shall keep it sweet
By some strange art;
Wild honey I shall eat
When I eat my heart.

O honey cool and chaste
As clover's breath!
Sweet Heaven I shall taste
Before my death.

Elinor Wylie

Ad Finem

On the white throat of useless passion
That scorched my soul with its burning breath
I clutched my hands in murderous fashion,
And held them close in a grip of death;
For why should I fan, or feed with fuel,
A love that showed me but blank despair?
So my hold was firm, and my grasp was cruel—
I meant to strangle it then and there!

I thought it was dead. But with no warning,
It rose from its grave last night, and came
And stood by my bed til the early morning
And over and over it spoke your name.
Its throat was red where my hands had held it;
It burned my brow with its scorching breath;
And I knew the moment my eyes beheld it,
'A love like this can know no death.'

For just one kiss that your lips have given
In the lost and beautiful past to me,
I would gladly barter my hopes of Heaven
And all the bliss of Eternity.
For never a joy are the angels keeping,
To lay at my feet in Paradise,

Like that into your strong arms creeping,
And looking into your love-lit eyes.

I know, in the way that sins are reckoned,
This thought is a sin of the deepest dye;
But I know too if an angel beckoned,
Standing close by the Throne on High,
And you, adown by the gates infernal,
Should open your loving arms and smile,
I would turn my back on things supernal,
To lay on your breast a little while.

To know for an hour you were mine completely—
Mine in body and soul, my own—
I would bear unending tortures sweetly,
With not a murmur and not a moan.
A lighter sin or lesser error
Might change through hope or fear divine;
But there is no fear, and hell has no terror,
To change or alter a love like mine.

Ella Wheeler Wilcox

Wild nights— Wild nights!

Wild nights—Wild nights!
Were I with thee
Wild nights should be
Our luxury!

Futile—the Winds—
To a Heart in port—
Done with the Compass—
Done with the Chart!

Rowing in Eden—
Ah, the Sea!
Might I but moor—Tonight—
In thee!

Emily Dickinson

Night of Sleepless Love

We two, the night ahead, the full moon looming:
I began to weep while you laughed.
Your scorn became a god, and my complaints
were little doves and moments in a chain.

We two, the night ahead, crystal of pain,
and you wept over deep and distant things.
My sorrow was a clump of agony
resting on your fragile heart of sand.

The dawn drew us together on the bed.
Our mouths were waiting near the frozen spout
of blood that spilled forth in an endless flow.

The sun came through the shuttered balcony
and the coral of life opened its branch,
and settled here upon my shrouded heart.

Federico García Lorca

The Meeting

We started speaking,
Looked at each other, then turned away.
The tears kept rising to my eyes.
But I could not weep.
I wanted to take your hand
But my hand trembled.
You kept counting the days
Before we should meet again.
But both of us felt in our hearts
That we parted for ever and ever.
The ticking of the little clock filled the quiet room.
'Listen,' I said. 'It is so loud,
Like a horse galloping on a lonely road,
As loud as a horse galloping past in the night.'
You shut me up in your arms.
But the sound of the clock stifled our hearts' beating.
You said, 'I cannot go: all that is living of me
Is here for ever and ever.'
Then you went.
The world changed. The sound of the clock grew fainter,
Dwindled away, became a minute thing.
I whispered in the darkness. 'If it stops, I shall die.'

Katherine Mansfield

Where does such tenderness come from?

Where does such tenderness come from?
These aren't the first curls
I've wound around my finger—
I've kissed lips darker than yours.

The sky is washed and dark
(Where does such tenderness come from?)
Other eyes have known
and shifted away from my eyes.

But I've never heard words like this
in the night
(Where does such tenderness come from?)
with my head on your chest, rest.

Where does this tenderness come from?
And what will I do with it? Young
stranger, poet, wandering through town,
you and your eyelashes—longer than anyone's.

Marina Tsvetaeva
(translated by Ilya Kaminsky)

Extract from
Two Loves

And lo! within the garden of my dream
I saw two walking on a shining plain
Of golden light. The one did joyous seem
And fair and blooming, and a sweet refrain
Came from his lips; he sang of pretty maids
And joyous love of comely girl and boy,
His eyes were bright, and 'mid the dancing blades
Of golden grass his feet did trip for joy;
And in his hand he held an ivory lute
With strings of gold that were as maidens' hair,
And sang with voice as tuneful as a flute,
And round his neck three chains of roses were.
But he that was his comrade walked aside;
He was full sad and sweet, and his large eyes
Were strange with wondrous brightness, staring wide
With gazing; and he sighed with many sighs
That moved me, and his cheeks were wan and white
Like pallid lilies, and his lips were red
Like poppies, and his hands he clenched tight,

And yet again unclenched, and his head
Was wreathed with moon-flowers pale as lips of death.
A purple robe he wore, o'erwrought in gold
With the device of a great snake, whose breath
Was fiery flame: which when I did behold
I fell a-weeping, and I cried, 'Sweet youth,
Tell me why, sad and sighing, thou dost rove
These pleasent realms? I pray thee speak me sooth
What is thy name?' He said, 'My name is Love.'
Then straight the first did turn himself to me
And cried, 'He lieth, for his name is Shame,
But I am Love, and I was wont to be
Alone in this fair garden, till he came
Unasked by night; I am true Love, I fill
The hearts of boy and girl with mutual flame.'
Then sighing, said the other, 'Have thy will,
I am the love that dare not speak its name.'

Lord Alfred Douglas

Passion

Some have won a wild delight,
    By daring wilder sorrow;
Could I gain thy love to-night,
    I'd hazard death to-morrow.

Could the battle-struggle earn
    One kind glance from thine eye,
How this withering heart would burn,
    The heady fight to try!

Welcome nights of broken sleep,
    And days of carnage cold,
Could I deem that thou wouldst weep
    To hear my perils told.

Tell me, if with wandering bands
    I roam full far away,
Wilt thou, to those distant lands,
    In spirit ever stray?

Wild, long, a trumpet sounds afar;
    Bid me, bid me go
Where Seik and Briton meet in war,
    On Indian Sutlej's flow.

Blood has dyed the Sutlej's waves
    With scarlet stain, I know;
Indus' borders yawn with graves,
    Yet, command me go!

Charlotte Brontë

Stanza

Oh, come to me in dreams, my love!
I will not ask a dearer bliss;
Come with the starry beams, my love,
And press mine eyelids with thy kiss.

'Twas thus, as ancient fables tell,
Love visited a Grecian maid,
Till she disturbed the sacred spell,
And woke to find her hopes betrayed.

But gentle sleep shall veil my sight,
And Psyche's lamp shall darkling be,
When, in the visions of the night,
Thou dost renew thy vows to me.

Then come to me in dreams, my love,
I will not ask a dearer bliss;
Come with the starry beams, my love,
And press mine eyelids with thy kiss.

Mary Shelley

Come Fill the Cup

Come, fill the cup, and in the fire of spring
Your winter garment of repentance fling.
The bird of time has but a little way
To flutter—and the bird is on the wing.

Omar Khayyam

Love Song

How can I keep my soul in me, so that
it doesn't touch your soul? How can I raise
it high enough, past you, to other things?
I would like to shelter it, among remote
lost objects, in some dark and silent place
that doesn't resonate when your depths resound.
Yet everything that touches us, me and you,
takes us together like a violin's bow,
which draws one voice out of two separate strings.
Upon what instrument are we two spanned?
And what musician holds us in his hand?
Oh sweetest song.

Rainer Maria Rilke

The Ship Sunk in Love

Should love's heart rejoice unless I burn?
For my heart is love's dwelling.
If you will burn your house, burn it, love!
Who will say,
'It's not allowed'?
Burn this house thoroughly!
The lover's house improves with fire.
From now on I will make burning my aim;
From now on I will make burning my aim,
for I am like the candle: burning
only makes me brighter.
Abandon sleep tonight;
traverse for one night
the region of the sleepless.
Look upon these lovers who have become
distraught and like moths have died
in union with the one beloved.
Look upon this ship of God's creatures
and see how it is sunk in love.

Rumi

Rumi
(1207–1273)

Scholar, theologian and Sufi mystic, Rumi was a thirteenth-century Persian poet who authored tens of thousands of verses, mostly written in the final 12 years of his life. Rumi's works have long been revered in Persian literature but twentieth-century translations of his poetry have led to worldwide popularity with audiences admiring his thoughts on love, philosophy and the divine communicated in a concise, melodic and sensuous style.

Rumi was greatly influenced by Shams Tabrizi, a poet and spiritual instructor who he met in 1244, and it was after this time that his prolific outpouring of poems began. They are collected in two major works: the six-volume *Spiritual Couplets*, which is often called the greatest mystical poem in world literature, and *Great Work*, which was named in honour of his mentor, Shams.

Throughout his writing, Rumi speaks of love as vehicle for humanity's deepest and most universal longings – for connection, with God and one another, and the quest for inner peace. 'The Ship Sunk in Love' is one example of his use of sensual, and even sexually charged language, to describe this love, which can be interpreted on as many levels as the reader wishes.

He Is More Than a Hero

He is more than a hero
he is a god in my eyes—
the man who is allowed
to sit beside you—he

who listens intimately
to the sweet murmur of
your voice, the enticing

laughter that makes my own
heart beat fast. If I meet
you suddenly, I can't

speak—my tongue is broken;
a thin flame runs under
my skin; seeing nothing,

hearing only my own ears
drumming, I drip with sweat;
trembling shakes my body

and I turn paler than
dry grass. At such times
death isn't far from me.

Sappho

Extract from The Princess: Now Sleeps the Crimson Petal

Now sleeps the crimson petal, now the white;
Nor waves the cypress in the palace walk;
Nor winks the gold fin in the porphyry font.
The firefly wakens; waken thou with me.

Now droops the milk-white peacock like a ghost,
And like a ghost she glimmers on to me.

Now lies the Earth all Danaë to the stars,
And all thy heart lies open unto me.

Now slides the silent meteor on, and leaves
A shining furrow, as thy thoughts in me.

Now folds the lily all her sweetness up,
And slips into the bosom of the lake.
So fold thyself, my dearest, thou, and slip
Into my bosom and be lost in me.

Alfred, Lord Tennyson

The Sick Rose

O Rose thou art sick.
The invisible worm,
That flies in the night
In the howling storm:

Has found out thy bed
Of crimson joy:
And his dark secret love
Does thy life destroy.

William Blake